HOW TO GET READY TO BE A PARENT —

And Be the Best Mom or Dad
You Can Possibly Be.

— A Life Guide —

HOW TO GET READY TO BE A PARENT —

And Be the Best Mom or Dad
You Can Possibly Be.

— A Life Guide —

Dr. Suzanne J. Gelb, Ph.D., J.D.

FIRST EDITION

All rights reserved. This book or any portion thereof may not be reproduced or used in any manner whatsoever without the express written permission of the publisher except for the use of brief quotations in a book review.

Copyright © 2019 Dr. Suzanne J. Gelb, Ph.D., J.D.

Manufactured in the United States of America.

ISBN-13: 978-1-950764-02-0
ISBN-10: 1-950764-02-8

www.DrSuzanneGelb.com

CONTENTS

Disclaimer   xi

INTRODUCTION

Learn To Navigate the Parenting Journey, Learn To Relax Into It and Enjoy It Fully.   1

WHAT'S INSIDE AND HOW TO USE THIS GUIDE.   4

STEP 1

How Are You Feeling and What Are Your Concerns?   5

STEP 2

What Are Your Parenting Intentions?   8

STEP 3

What Are Your Patterns?   12

STEP 4

Changing Your Patterns.   16

STEP 5

Soothing Your Fears.   20

STEP 6

Make a Plan.   24

STEP 7

Gathering Support. (Who's on Your Team?)   28

10 Frequently Asked Questions From Parents-To-Be.   30

A FEW FINAL WORDS

Parenting Can Be a Challenge, but It Doesn't Have To Be Complicated.   84

WHAT'S NEXT?

Resources To Keep Learning and Growing.   85

ABOUT THE AUTHOR   99

OTHER BOOKS BY THE AUTHOR   100

INDEX   102

DISCLAIMER

This book is a tool that can help you to become the BEST version of yourself, so you can be the BEST parent you can possibly be.

This book contains educational exercises and tips drawn from my career in the field of emotional wellness with over 30 years of experience. This book is for informational purposes only, and is not intended to diagnose or treat any illness, nor is it a substitute for professional or psychological advice, diagnosis, or treatment. Always consult a qualified health care professional before engaging in any new, self-help resource (such as this one) and with questions you may have about your health and wellbeing.

Any case material that may be alluded to in this book, including in articles, or in interviews [see Resources section] does not constitute guarantees of similar outcomes for the reader. No results can be promised, since everyone's personal development path is unique. Names and details have been changed for privacy.

Links inside this book to external websites are for informational purposes only. Linking does not imply endorsement of or affiliation with that site, its content, or any product or service it may offer.

All link URLs in this book are current at the time of printing. Link URLs may fail at some point if the page has been deleted or moved. The author assumes no responsibility or liability for broken links.

This concludes the disclaimer portion of this book.

Thank you. Enjoy this Guide ... and enjoy your life..

INTRODUCTION

Learn To Navigate the Parenting Journey, Learn To Relax Into It and Enjoy It Fully

Welcome to The Life Guide on How To Get Ready To Be A Parent.

Congratulations are in order! You're going to be a parent!

If you picked up a copy of this Guide, chances are, you might be feeling ...

—Incredibly **happy and excited** ... but uncertain about how to prepare for the adventure ahead. ("I'm ready! But, um, what's next?")

—Completely **anxious and overwhelmed**. ("Whoa! I'm NOT ready for this!")

—**Worried** that somehow, you're going to do parenting "wrong." That you'll repeat the same mistakes as your parents or peers. ("I don't want to be like ... so-and-so.")

—**Worried** that becoming a parent will "change" you. That you'll become someone "else." Someone you don't like. ("I don't want to become one of those exhausted, irritable, resentful parents, like ... so-and-so.")

—**Worried** that when your family grows, your relationship with your partner will change. ("Will he get jealous or feel left out, if I'm spending lots of time with the baby?" "How will our sexual relationship be different after our child is born — will she still be interested?")

Parenthood is a huge life commitment. It's no surprise that you may be feeling ... a lot of feelings!

But whatever you're feeling, the good news is: **parenting is not an unsolvable mystery**. In fact, it's much less complex than many people think.

Your job is simply to teach your child right from wrong, while ensuring that they feel completely secure in your love. (Your unconditional love.)

After moving through this Life Guide, you can be better equipped to navigate the parenting journey — so that you can **relax into and enjoy it, fully**.

If you're already a parent and expecting another child, consider this a quick reference guide and refresher course.

Or perhaps you want to do things differently this time around. It's never too late to learn to do better. To bring out the absolute best in your child(ren) and in yourself.

Before we dive in — a logistical note, for couples:

If you're part of a couple, it's a good idea to work through this Guide separately, each on your own, and then come together to share your responses to each question.

This can help you to see where you're aligned, and where your values and parenting styles might be diverging.

Noticing those places where you diverge — early — is so important. It means you'll have a chance to address those differences before they turn into nasty fights, or a pattern of inconsistent parenting, later down the line.

It's up to BOTH of you to give your child the gift of a unified parenting team.

What's Inside and How To Use This Guide

Inside this Life Guide, you'll find a series of steps to guide you through preparing for the joyous experience of being a mom or dad.

Some steps include fill-in-the-blank worksheets.

Other steps will help you uplift your self-talk and identify helpful (and not-so-helpful) parenting patterns already at work in you.

Plus, a self-care planning worksheet is included.

Each step is designed to help you become the BEST version of yourself, so you can be the BEST parent you can possibly be.

The Contents page of the book gave you a peek at what's ahead.

STEP 1

How Are You Feeling and What Are Your Concerns?

As a psychologist and life coach, I almost always begin my sessions with a simple emotional "check-in," to help clients connect with their feelings.

Why start there? Because it's difficult to manage your feelings and deal with stress when you don't really know what those feelings are.

Start Here, With a Writing Exercise To Get All Those Feelings Out.

Try not to over-think your answers or worry if they sound "silly" or "inappropriate." **Self-criticism is never ok.**

Just express whatever you feel.

When it comes to being a parent:

One thing I'm really excited about is

_____

_____

One thing I'm pretty "freaked out" about is

_____

_____

One thing that's a constant source of worry is

_____

_____

One thing my parents did that I'm determined NOT to repeat is

_____

_____

One tradition my parents taught me that I'd like to pass along to my child is

_____

_____

One area where I really need support is

_____

_____

Overall, right now, I'm feeling

_____

_____

Naming your feelings isn't the same as "managing" them — but it's the first step.

We'll talk about **what to "do" with all those feelings**, a bit later in this Guide.

Next up: Let's talk about **your intentions as a parent** — the values that you wish to pass on to your child.

STEP 2

What Are Your Parenting Intentions?

If you've ever taken a yoga class, your teacher probably invited you to "set an intention" for your practice.

Your "intention" might be:

— A **dedication** to someone you love ("I'm dedicating my practice to Grandma Muriel.")

Or it might be:

—An **expression of care** for those around you ("With every stretch, I will imagine sending kindness out into the universe.")

Or it might be:

—Something **physical and practical** ("My intention is to break a sweat ... and feel good!")

Setting an intention might sound "weird" or "woo-woo" if you're unfamiliar with the concept. But it's really no different than writing your wedding vows, drawing up a contract for a client, or writing a mission statement for your business.

It's about **making a commitment to your child** — with clear values and lessons that you wish to pass down.

Not sure what your intentions are?

Fill in the Blanks in This Writing Exercise, and Start To Explore …

I define being a "good person" as

_____

_____

I define leading a "successful life" as

_____

_____

I define a "happy home" as

_____

_____

Some of the values that I'd like to pass down to my child are

_____

_____

I want my child to know that no matter what, he / she deserves

_____

_____

I want my child to know that no matter what, they will always have

_____

_____

Growing up, I want my child to be challenged to

_____

_____

Growing up, I want my child to be exposed to

_____

_____

Ultimately, I want my child to grow up into the kind of person who

_____

_____

Now that you've written down a few of your values and hopes for your child, let's look at some of the **things that might BLOCK you from honoring those intentions**.

Specifically: the unresolved feelings and patterns that can hold you back from being the best possible parent for your child.

STEP 3

What Are Your Patterns?

Every parent has certain "patterns" — helpful patterns and unhelpful ones, too.

A **helpful pattern** might be:

—Reading your child a bedtime story every night, because that's what happened in your childhood home.

An **unhelpful pattern** might be:

—Not enforcing household rules, or allowing your (adorable, but uncooperative) child to manipulate you, because you don't like saying "no."

These patterns didn't materialize out of thin air. They're (primarily) a response to the way YOU were raised.

In order to become the most effective parent you can possibly be, it can be helpful to **understand where your patterns came from** — why you behave the way you do.

Here's a pair of true stories that illustrate how unhelpful parenting patterns can originate, and how they can create trouble ... unless they're identified and resolved.

The Meaning of NO: Katie's Dad's Story

Katie's dad was a middle child. His siblings got much more attention than he did, and he felt like he never got what he wanted.

So when 3-year-old Katie wailed, "I want that," her dad said, "No, you can't have a cupcake, it's bedtime." Then he remembered his deprived youth, and thought, "Poor kid." He identified with his daughter's gripe. Not wanting her to suffer like he had, he caved in. He rationalized, "She's just a kid, I'll teach her to cooperate and respect my 'No,' later."

Unfortunately, "later" rarely comes, and the absence of positive discipline can be costly. When Katie was 4, her parents came to see me and complained that "she's uncontrollable."

That's what can happen when undisciplined children reach age 4 or 5. They do not understand the meaning of "no".

*I introduced Katie's parents to **positive discipline**. This means **firm, fair guidance that is applied with love**. It also includes **reasonable rules** for behavior that are enforced, along with **appropriate consequences** for non-compliance.*

Fortunately, this mom and dad, who had both avoided disciplining Katie because of their deprived upbringing, were extremely conscientious about applying positive discipline. In time, they were able to reverse Katie's unruly behavior.

The Reason for the Rules: Charlie's Mother's Story

When 6-year-old Charlie asked his mother, "Why do I have to take out the garbage?" she yelled, "Because I said so!" Then she punished Charlie for questioning her.

This is the exact type of overly strict parenting that Charlie's mother experienced when she was a child.

*The problem with her **authoritarian** style of parenting is that **it wasn't teaching Charlie to make positive choices**. The only reason he obeyed was to avoid punishment. When no one was watching, he would rebel and misbehave.*

When Charlie's mom came to see me because of his behavioral problems, we discussed how her parenting style was replicating what she had experienced as a child.

She realized that she needed to change her parenting style — from overly strict (like her parents' approach) to more positive — a style that would be based on positive discipline.

With that in place, the next time Charlie asked her a "Why do I have to ..." question, she took a deep breath, and patiently explained.

*Not surprisingly, Charlie began cooperating. **When children are given a reason as to why they need to do something — a reason that makes sense to them — they're far more likely to cooperate.***

Identifying one's parenting patterns can take time — and sometimes professional input might be appropriate, particularly if we're not aware our own unconscious patterns.

If you decide that you'd like to work with a professional, it's wise to follow through and take that step. Your child is counting on you.

But for now ...

Pay attention to instances when you experience something that triggers an exaggerated emotional response (Like: "Whoa! I'm SO mad / sad / anxious / frustrated, even though this isn't a huge deal.")

Those moments are clues, pointing to possible unresolved emotions and unhelpful patterns. Notice them. **Jot them down in a journal.** In time, the patterns are likely to become clearer.

Next? We'll explore **how to change those unhelpful patterns**, once you've identified them.

STEP 4

Changing Your Patterns

No matter how you were raised, and whether you feel your parents did a "good job" or "not-so-great job," you have an opportunity to do better, with your child.

Not just an opportunity — *a responsibility.*

You Can Start To Reframe Your Negative Patterns and Commit to Making Changes for the Better ... With These Affirmations.

Even though my parents did

_____

_____

I know how to do better.

I can

_____

_____

Even though

_____

_____

happened in my childhood home, in my home, we will do better.

I can give my child

_____

_____

Even though I've always had a tough time with

_____

_____

I have the power to change.

From now on, I will

_____

_____

Even though it's hard for me to

_____

_____

I know that my child deserves the BEST version of me. The BEST parent I can be.

From now on, I will

_____

_____

Uncovering Subconscious Patterns: Rachel's Story.

When Rachel came to see me, she was frustrated because of her love-hate feelings and explosive reactions towards her family.

"When my kids cooperate," she explained, "I love them. But when they misbehave, I get mad at them and don't like them."

This love-hate relationship extended to her husband as well. When he complimented her, she felt loving toward him. When he disagreed and she didn't get her way, she got angry, whined and complained about how much she disliked him.

"I feel bad about my verbal abuse towards my family," she said. "And I feel guilty for not liking them."

Rachel wanted to know why she felt this way and where her feelings came from.

I learned more about her in follow-up meetings. Together, we discovered that she had a lot of pent-up anger and grief about her own upbringing. Her parents usually said "no" to anything she wanted, without explanation. When she asked "Why?" she was told, "It's none of your business," or "Don't talk back!"

It was traumatic for young Rachel to hear these harsh words, and she felt angry, sad and rejected for much of her childhood.

I explained to adult Rachel that since it's not possible to be consciously aware of all our childhood experiences, we often store these memories in our subconscious.

And sometimes — when an adult has feelings similar to those that are stored the subconscious — the stored material resurfaces and we become aware of it.

Rachel's strong feelings seemed to have surfaced from her subconscious. They were causing her to behave (at times) like a resentful child, who still wanted to know why she couldn't get her way, and wanted to punish and get even with anyone who wasn't treating her the way she wanted.

I helped Rachel heal the feelings from her past that had caused her to become controlling and retaliatory. This helped her to relate more positively to her family.

...

A strong feeling that many parents and parents-to-be face is ... **fear**.

Next: we'll explore **what to "do" with that feeling**, so it doesn't fester inside, overwhelm, or cause you to become stuck.

STEP **5**

Soothing Your Fears.

Taking on a new responsibility almost always triggers some fear.

And parenting is a BIG responsibility, so it's understandable if it sometimes triggers a BIG amount of fear!

But fear doesn't have to overwhelm you, or stop you from doing what needs to be done. You can learn to manage it. This is a very important skill to learn, because **fear is a natural human response that's meant to work FOR, not against, us**.

So, the sooner you learn how to manage it, the better for you — and your child.

Try This Exercise:

Using the blank spaces below, **write down every fear you can think of and a sensible, potential solution to it**.

Keep repeating these three lines until you've worked through every fear you can think of — even if it's a very long list!

When it comes to being a parent, I am really scared of

_____

_____

But when I'm feeling scared, I don't need to let it hold me back, or stop me from doing what I need to do.

I can do something productive and pro-active, like

_____

_____

Once you've covered every fear you can think of, if you're still feeling a bit uneasy, try this affirmation:

I am capable.

I am kind.

I can take beautiful care of myself and others. Everything is going to work out.

Overcoming Fear: Joey's Mom's Story.

Joey's mom was very fearful of letting him go into the deep end of a swimming pool.

When Joey's swim teacher took her young students to the deep end of the pool to practice treading water, 6-year-old Joey stayed behind. "My mom doesn't let me go into the deep end," he said tearfully.

After swim class, Joey's mother told his teacher, "It's too dangerous!" She then cancelled Joey's swim lessons.

"This mom means well," thought the instructor, "But her overprotectiveness is counterproductive. Joey won't learn to swim properly and he'll grow up being afraid of the water."

The instructor was right. In the months that followed, Joey refused to go into the ocean, and he wouldn't play under the water sprinkler with his friends.

Joey's mother soon realized that she was instilling fear, instead of confidence, in her son. This concerned her greatly, and it was the reason she came to see me.

"Joey's not only afraid of the water," she said, "He's afraid to try new experiences."

Although Joey's mom was still deeply concerned about her son's safety, she also wanted to know why she was so scared of letting him into the deep end of a pool.

In time, I learned that this caring, devoted mother had experienced several traumatic incidents in her life where she felt out of control and panicked. In particular, when Joey was 3, he fell into a neighbor's pool and nearly drowned. His mom blamed herself, "I was supposed to be watching him. For a second, I didn't ... and he fell in." Several years later, she was still feeling anxious and guilty over the pool incident and other traumas.

Once Joey's mother identified the distressing incidents that gave rise to her excessive fears she was able to understand why her fears were so intense. She then dealt with the pent-up feelings related to these past incidents, that were fueling her present behavior with Joey. Resolving this, helped her to parent more positively.

While she's still vigilant about Joey's welfare, she now accepts that scratches and bruises are part of childhood. As she explains, "I share with Joey that my concern is for his safety, not because I think he's accident-prone or incapable of doing some activities. I'm learning to let him explore the world — and I signed him up for swim lessons again!"

STEP **6**

Make a Plan

Your biggest job, in the months leading up to your child's arrival, is to take extra-special care of your body and emotions, and to avoid getting stressed — or, if you do get stressed, to find healthy ways to release all that pent-up emotion.

Self-Care = a Way To Care for Your Child, Even Before He or She Is Born.

Turn the page, to find a planning worksheet that can help you make self-care a high priority, every day, and every week.

SELF-CARE PLANNING WORKSHEET

Review the worksheet on the next page.

Grab a sheet of paper and write by hand (rather than type) the seven affirmations exactly as you see them on the page. As you write, think thoroughly about the words that you're writing.

Then, fill in the blanks with self-care practices that feel nourishing ... and realistic.

(For example: *"Taking a 5-minute dance break while listening to happy pop music"* might be doable. *"Signing up for a 12-week dance class with training 3 nights a week"* might not.)

Put your completed worksheet somewhere visible, where you'll see it every day — like on the refrigerator.

I suggest filling out this worksheet once a week, starting fresh.

To keep things simple, write down just *one* self-care practice to try, for each category. Don't overwhelm yourself with too many "assignments." This is about *releasing* stress — not creating more!

Above all: treat yourself with **gentleness, patience and care** — the same gentleness, patience and care that you will provide for your child.

WORKSHEET

THIS WEEK ...

BODY: To take better care of my body, I will

_____

_____

_____

MIND: To inspire and stimulate my mind, I will

_____

_____

_____

EMOTIONS: To release pent-up emotions, I will

_____

_____

_____

HOME: To organize and prepare my home, I will

_____

_____

_____

PARTNERSHIP: To strengthen my bond with my partner, I will

_____

_____

_____

FUN: And just for fun, I will

_____

_____

_____

STEP 7

Gathering Support. (Who's on Your Team?)

That old cliche — "It takes a village to raise a child" — is absolutely true.

And as a parent, you are at the center of your child's life, which means: you design the village.

You'll need support before and after your child arrives. Seek it out and accept it.

In doing so, you can become a well-rested and healthy parent, able to manage stress much better, and make better choices.

You'll also be modeling good self-care for your child — and when they're a bit older, they'll notice, and be inspired by your example.

So, Who's on Your Team?

Start by making a list of all the people who love you, care about you, and want to help you.

Make a commitment (with yourself) to keep nourishing those relationships, so they don't fade away.

Some of the people who love me, care about me, and want to help me are:

_____

_____

_____

_____

_____

_____

_____

_____

_____

_____

_____

_____

In addition to nourishing your relationships with family and friends, you can find support from professional resources, too, if you feel you need it.

Here Are 10 Questions That Parents-to-Be (First, Second or Third Child) Have Typically Asked When They Reached Out to Me for Professional Support.

Each question is followed by a general response, plus an exercise that ties it all together.

Question No. 1 — Weight-Gain

Getting Back in Shape Post-Birth

This might sound vain and superficial," says a mother who is soon to have her first child. "But I'm used to exercising a lot and being in fantastic shape.

I'm worried that after giving birth I'll be so flabby, and I'll feel discouraged by what I see in the mirror.

Response:

Your question is understandable and you're not alone. One of the major challenges that a new mother can face after pregnancy, is getting her body in shape.

Achieving this goal nurtures a mother's self-esteem. This is so important because then she feels good about herself as she tackles the responsibilities of caring for a baby.

Your husband's support can make a big difference during this time. When a father is sensitive to a mother's needs after she gives birth, his understanding and encouragement can helped the mother survive the task of getting her body fit.

So enlist your husband's support. And as he helps with the baby, let him know how much you appreciate his help, so that you can start exercising again.

Be sure to nurture yourself during this time of extra demands.

For example:

Pick a suitable time where you can stop what you're doing, just for a moment. Take a deep breath. This can be so refreshing.

Remember that your child is likely to mirror you. As you become confident, peaceful and feel good about yourself, this is likely to have a positive effect on your child.

Self-Nurturing Exercise:

Affirm

I, _____ commit to doing the following every day for at least one week:

At least three times today, I will stop what I'm doing and take a deep breath to refresh myself.

Later, on the same day, write down how you felt before and after you did the breathing exercise.

Before I took a deep breath, I was feeling

_____

_____

_____

After I took a deep breath, I felt

_____

_____

_____

Question No. 2 — First Year of Life: Stay Home or Go To Work?

How Moms Can Feel Confident About Parenting in any Setting

I'm thinking about having my first child. I'm not sure whether to be a stay-at-home mom once my baby is born, or whether to work.

Economically, my husband and I can afford for me to stay home (for a while, anyway), but I'm worried about being criticized or stigmatized for not working.

But if I return to work some time after about having the baby, I'm afraid that being away from my baby for many hours, is not best for my baby's development.

Can you help with this difficult decision of whether to be home with the baby, or go back to work?

Response:

Ideally, if you could be home for at least the first year of your child's life — when essential bonding can take place between you and your child — that could be very positive for your child.

The maternal nurturing that occurs during the first year of a child's life, and the effect this can have on a child's future development, is very significant.

A baby's future self-esteem, confidence and social skills are rooted in the foundation created by these early experiences.

As you nurture your child through this first year, be sure to team up with your husband and if possible, share parenting responsibilities with him.

If he can help with childcare, and make it a priority to spend quality time with the baby, then you will know that you can count on him for support.

This can enable you to give your best to your child and have confidence in your parenting skills.

Follow-Up Question

"What if, because of career and economics, I find myself in a situation where both I and my husband need to work, after the baby is born?"

Response:

In that situation, at the very least, you'd want to be sure that you select only trusted adults to care for your baby in your absence.

In addition, it's important that these caregivers share your approach to parenting, so that there is consistency in the care that your baby receives. Everyone's on the same page, so to speak.

That said, some moms who work during the first year feel quite conflicted as they think:

"I should be with my child."

On the other hand, some moms who need to be at work, but choose to stay home with their kids, feel conflicted as they think:

"I should be at work."

Parents have creatively solved this conflict in various ways including:

—Some moms have been able to solve the conflict of needing to work, but wanting to be with their child, by working at home.

—Others, who have worked for businesses that have a nursery in the office building, have taken their baby to work. They have been able to frequently visit their infants in the nursery.

—Some moms have been able to reduce their work hours from full-time to part time.

They also have peace of mind that when they are at work, knowing that their baby is in the capable, trusted care of their father or another reliable adult.

—Sometimes the father is able to take on an extra job. This would allow the mother to stay home on a part-time or full-time basis, at least during the first year.

—In other instances, the father does more of the household chores than he used to, prior to the birth of newborn.

For example, he may do more cleaning than he used to. He also may do more cooking, and / or share more quality time with their other children

A Message From Dr. Gelb to Mothers Who Work

If you combine mothering and work, be careful not to get caught up in work demands and business.

That happens quite often. And before you know it, deadlines, never-ending To-Do lists, and rushing, have become your way of life.

And your child? Doesn't see much of you.

A basis of a child's self-esteem and self-confidence is that they feel important. They need to feel that they are a priority to their parents.

Self-Assessment

Reflect on the following questions. Record your answers in a journal.

For parents who are thinking about having a child, or getting ready to have a child:

Will I be able to allocate enough time to spend with my child?

_____

_____

_____

_____

If not, what do I need to do/how can I make it possible to spend more time with my child?

_____

_____

_____

_____

For parents who are already have a child/children:

Do I spend enough time with my child/children?

_____

_____

_____

_____

If not, what do I need to do/how can I make it possible to spend more time with my child/children?

_____

_____

_____

_____

Question No. 3 — Single Parent

How a Single Parent Can Raise Happy, Well-Adjusted, Successful Children

In a few months, my first child will be born. My spouse passed away not long ago. This was completely unexpected, and I'll be raising my son on my own.

I've heard that kids who are raised by a single parent suffer low self-esteem. Is this true?

Also, even though it's not my fault that my child will grow up without a father, I feel really guilty that he is not going to grow up in a home where he is loved and cared for by two parents.

Response:

First, I'm so sorry for your loss.

And, No, I don't subscribe to the theory that children who are raised by a single parent are inevitably worse off.

Although the ideal is for a child to grow up a stable household, with two solid parents, in my professional experience it is entirely possible for single parents to create stable, happy homes in which their children can thrive.

A few things to watch out for:

1. Being Overprotective

Some parents who have sustained a loss such as you have, or suffered a painful breakup, feel lonely and try to keep their children near.

This tends to be especially the case when the children are older (younger kids tend to be more under the parent's wing anyway.)

Say for example, when your son is 11 years old, he wants to sleep over at an older boy's house. You say "No" because you think you're protecting him. But in actuality, deep down you're wanting him to stay home so you'll have company.

This may be hard to imagine, especially since your son isn't even born yet… but I have seen this type of scenario play out over and over again in my 30+ years of working with families. It's important that you know about this, so you can watch out for it.

On the flip side, say your 11-year-old son really wants to spend the night at his older friend's home, but feels guilty for leaving you alone. That's not healthy either.

Single parents need to be especially mindful of letting their children to be children.

These parents would be wise to create their own network of adult companions. Then they won't be looking to their children to be their friends.

Instead, they will feel comfortable encouraging their children to socialize with their (the children's) own friends.

2. Being a Super-Parent

Another way that single parents often try to make up for the absence of a second parent is by **trying to be both mom and dad** for their child.

What typically ends up happening is that these parents **spread themselves too thin**, with **too much to do** and never enough time.

Ways to work around this:

—**Be realistic** about what are able to do for your child

—**Be easy** on yourself for what you can't do.

—**Don't complain** about how overloaded you are. Instead, ask for help (from trusted family members, neighbors, or parents of your child's friends.)

—Be well-**organized**.

—**Prioritize** the items on your To-Do list.

—**Delegate** tasks to help lighten your workload.

Guilt-Free Parenting

As for feeling guilty that your child will not grow up with a father, some things to watch out for:

—Sometimes, when one parent is absent, the other parent has to work a lot, essentially trying to earn the equivalent of two incomes. So the working parent spends even less time with their child.

End result: The parent feels guilty for **two losses** that heir children are experiencing:

- Loss of the other parent

- Loss of time with the working parent

—To make up for the losses that these parents feel their children were experiencing, what often happens is that the single parent becomes **super lenient** and **shies away from positive discipline.**

Children who are raised without positive discipline, tend to be disrespectful and unruly.

Sometimes counseling is needed to assist the parent to resolve their guilt. After that, the parent is likely to be ready to implement sound parenting skills.

This means teaching a child how to behave respectfully and appropriately by establishing reasonable rules, along with consequences for non-compliance.

Follow-Up Question

"I'm worried that my son's development will be negatively affected by not having a dad. When he's old enough, I can teach him and be a role model for how to treat a woman, but I don't see how I can build his confidence as a man. This really worries me."

Response:

When the time is right, you could consider reaching out to other dependable adults such as a relative or a family friend.

For example:

—If you have a brother, or a male cousin who you are close to, you could invite one or both of them to weekly family meals.

Then your son could bond with his uncle or relative, and is likely to enjoy the contact.

—Also, when you son is older, see if there is a sport that he might be interested in, such as baseball.

Then you could try to arrange for him to play under a male coach who you believe could be a healthy influence.

Fill in the Blanks in This Writing Exercise, and Start To Feel Good About the Parenting Journey Ahead ...

I define being a "successful single parent" as

_____

_____

_____

I define raising a "successful child" as

_____

_____

_____

I define a "happy, single parent home" as

_____

_____

_____

Now that you've written down a few of your definitions for raising a happy, successful child, commit to bringing those definitions to life, to making them a reality.

I commit to being the BEST version of myself, and the BEST single parent for my child that I can possibly be.

From now on, I will

_____

_____

_____

I commit to raising my son to be a person who his father would be proud of.

From now on, I will

_____

_____

_____

I commit to creating a home for my son in which he can thrive.

From now on, I will

_____

_____

_____

Question No. 4 — Developmental Milestones

How To Know if Your Child Is on Track, Developmentally (and Avoid Getting Consumed With Baby Books in Search of the Answer)

Soon a second child will join our family. I'm super excited, but I confess I'm dreading all those baby manuals.

With my first child, I was consumed by baby books, always searching for reassurance that my child was developing properly. I've never been good at trusting my gut.

It got to the point that I was so caught up with guidelines and checklists, that I had almost no time left to enjoy my baby. Seriously!

All this reading made me anxious especially when my child didn't conform to the time frames I was reading about — like when she wasn't smiling at the time the charts said she was supposed to.

My husband would say to me:

"Just relax, everything will work out."

That was good advice — because everything did work out.

But as a new mom, it was hard for me to sit back and not be preoccupied with how my child was developing.

How can I avoid getting caught up in the milestone frenzy when my second child arrives?

Response:

It is understandable that as a new parent, you would tend to be very vigilant and attentive to your child's needs.

But as you pointed out, you (and countless other parents) took things a step further — you became preoccupied with your child's developmental progression. And you felt anxious if it seemed that your child wasn't conforming.

A constructive way to bypass the milestone frenzy with your second child, would be to consult your pediatrician if you have questions about the timeframes that you're reading about.

This professional is likely to explain to you that those timeframes are averages and that just because a child might reach some developmental milestones sooner than average, and other milestones later than average, that doesn't mean the child is not still in the normal range.

A few things to pay attention to:

—Don't try to mold and correct your child's behavior to conform to some stringent guidelines that you read about.

This tends to be inhibiting, rather than supportive, because your child is not being allowed to develop in a natural way.

—Experts vary in their approaches to developmental milestones.

Some emphasize gross motor milestones such as crawling, walking and creeping up stairs, running etc.

Other experts emphasize intellectual and social development such as smiling responsively, cooing and grunting, etc.

—**Love and nurture your child**, and allow your child's development to happen in its **own pace and time.**

—**Personal touch,** primarily from parents or principal caregivers, is necessary for your child's development.

This could mean cuddling, holding, and stroking your child whenever possible.

This can facilitate bonding and allows a child to feel safe.

—**Trust your parental instincts.** As a mother, you have an innate maternal instinct to attend to your child's needs.

Some parents, without even knowing about conventional theories of development, naturally support their child's ability to grow and thrive.

The more you trust your instincts, the more you'll probably find that many of the recommendations that you read about in parenting books, articles, etc., are things that you are already doing.

Why is this significant?

It means that you just need to trust yourself.

—**Be a healthy role model.** Beginning at birth, and with each developmental stage that follows, your child is observing how you deal with your feelings and your life experiences.

This modeling has a powerful influence on a child's behavior because children emulate what they observe. This is how their character begins to form.

Now you can see why it is essential that parents are healthy role models and teach their children positive behavior.

No matter how anxious and consumed you were with baby books when you were raising your first child, you can do better with your second child.

Because your second child will be watching you — *and you want to be a healthy role model, not an anxious, insecure one.*

You Can Start To Release Your Anxiety and Commit to Being a Better Role Model ... With These Affirmations.

Even though I was anxious about my first child's development

_____

_____

I know how to do better.

With my second child, I can

_____

_____

Even though

_____

_____

happened when I was raising my first child, I can do better.

I can give my second child

_____

_____

Even though I've always had a tough time trusting my instincts

_____

_____

I can change and grow.

From this moment forward, I will

_____

_____

Question No. 5 — Sibling Rivalry

How To Prepare Your Child for the Arrival of a New Family Member

I have a four-year-old daughter with another one on the way. Cassie's a happy child, but I'm worried she'll feel ignored or jealous because we'll be giving her new sister so much attention.

How can I help my daughter adjust to her new sibling?"

Response:

It's really good that you're thinking about this now, before your second child arrives. Prevention is best because it's not uncommon for older siblings to *withdraw* or even to *act out*, in an effort to compete for their parents' attention, when a newborn arrives.

Parents can ease "sibling rivalry" by preparing their children for the arrival of a new family member, long before a baby is born.

—Talking about the pregnancy can be a good way to do this.

—Children can also track the development of the baby (for example: you could encourage your daughter to touch your belly and feel the baby kicking inside.)

—You can also read age-appropriate books to your child, that explain what happens after pregnancy and after birth.

—You can also prepare your daughter to adjust to her new sister by talking to her about how the family will care for the newborn .

Example:

"Cassie, soon, you me and Daddy will be taking care of your new sister.".

Including your daughter in this way can go a long way to ensuring that she don't feel replaced by your newborn. As such, her self-esteem can stay intact.

Try this exercise to help build your confidence that you can successfully help your daughter enjoy having a little sister.

Don't over think. Just express whatever comes to mind.

When it comes to helping my daughter welcome her new sister

One way I'm going to prepare her for the adjustment is

_____

_____

_____

Another way I'm going to prepare her for the adjustment is

_____

_____

_____

One way I'm going to make sure that she always feels included is

_____

_____

_____

Now that I know what to do to maintain Cassie's self-esteem, I feel

_____

_____

_____

_____

Question No. 6 — Sibling Rivalry

How To Help Older Siblings to Not Feel Jealous or Unimportant

I'm expecting another child (boy) soon, to join my two kids, age 10 and five. When my five-year-old daughter was born, her older brother resented her because of all the attention, visitors and presents she got.

My son would try to get my attention, but I had no patience because I was caring for the baby... so I'd get angry and snap at him. I felt really, really bad for exploding like this. Soon I'll have two older kids.

How can I make sure they don't feel jealous of their new sibling or unimportant?

Response:

Keep in mind that when a newborn consumes a parent's time and attention, this can be unsettling to a sibling ("siblings" in your situation).

In reality, however, it's possible for your older children to get even more attention than they did before the arrival of their new brother. How? If you include your older children in the infant's care.

Examples:

—They can help (in an age-appropriate way) with feeding or bathing the newborn.

—You could ask one of them, for example, to bring you a pacifier for the baby.

—You might ask your other child to find a toy for your newborn.

Encouraging your children to help and be involved in this way, can build their self-esteem and cause them to feel important ("I'm helping my mommy with my new brother!")

As everyone shares in caring for the infant, this involvement can foster a bond between family members, a sense of connectedness and togetherness.

Visualization Exercise

Find a quiet, private space in your home where you can take 3 to 5 minutes of quiet, uninterrupted time.

Sit comfortably and close your eyes.

Take a deep breath in.

Exhale.

Repeat (inhale, exhale).

Now, imagine that your new baby boy has recently arrived.

Picture your older children happily helping to care for their little brother.

Notice their eagerness and enthusiasm.

Notice the healthy pride they feel about being involved.

Visualize yourself:

—Praising them for being so helpful to you.

—Telling them how important they are to you, how much they matter to you.

Observe the beautiful closeness that is growing between your family members.

Spend a few moments enjoying this visualization.

When you're ready, open your eyes and adjust to the light in your environment.

Question No. 7 — Controlling Co-Parent

How To Minimize the Impact of Controlling Parents on Their Children

"My husband and will be new parents for the first time, early next year. We're having twins! We're so excited.

The problem is that he is controlling. I love him so much, but he always has to be to be right about everything. He never admits it if he makes a mistake or when he is wrong.

Sometimes we have heated arguments, but he always gets his way.

I'm worried how the twins will be affected when they see their dad trying to control me.

Will they grow up to be controlling, like their dad?"

Response:

When children see one parent controlling another, the impact can be significant.

What often happens is that these children tend to emulate the dominant parent.

Example:

Since your husband is controlling, the twins could be at risk for trying to control and manipulate (future) siblings, classmates or friends.

This could also carry over into their adult relationships. In other words, because your husband dominates you (or tries to), when the twins grow up, they may do the same to their spouses.

Something to watch out for:

A parent who controls his or her partner tends to control the children.

Positive discipline is not the same as control. Firm, fair consistent discipline applied with love is a teaching tool that helps children accomplish goals and understand consequences for choices.

Controlling behavior is punitive and degrading. It instills doubt and destroys confidence.

Follow-Up Question No. 1

"What caused my husband to become so controlling?"

Response:

There could be many reasons. Here are a few:

—Childhood conditioning

—Position in the family while growing up

—How one's parents treated each other

Follow-Up Question No. 2

My husband wasn't controlling when we dated. Why did the control only start after we were married?"

Response:

When two people are dating, they are typically on their best behavior.

This is why control issues can be dormant during dating.

Sometimes, only after the ink is dry do the true colors emerge.

Back to your initial question… will your twins grow up to be controlling?

Where a parents in a family is controlling, it is important to try to minimize the impact of this behavior on the children.

Controlling behavior in a marriage is a complex issue.

Remedies can range from self-help to professional counseling.

Examples of possible remedies:

—Standing up to the controller (if feasible).

To do this, the support of a counselor is often needed.

—Marriage counseling.

A marriage counselor can assist spouses to identify their roles in the relationship conflict.

It takes two people to create a problem.

The couple can also talk about what provokes them and learn better relating skills.

For this type of intervention to succeed both spouses must be committed to improving their marriage.

This may also lead to one or both spouses to realize that individual counseling (for their own personal issues) would be in order.

You indicated that your husband won't admit to being wrong. This suggests that he wouldn't be receptive to self-help or counseling. ("I don't need to do that, I'm not a control-freak!")

But sometimes, when there is a major change in life circumstances (like the pending arrival of your twins), people agree to doing things (like seeking counseling) that they otherwise wouldn't.

Getting Help.

Consider asking your husband if he would go with you to a couple's workshop.

He might surprise you and agree, but with this type of response:

"I'll go, but only to prove you're wrong. I'm not a control-freak."

Hopefully the workshop can be a start to resolving the control issues that are disrupting your marriage so that the twins are not negatively impacted.

Question No. 8 — Grandparents

How To Nurture Relationships With Ailing Grandparents

I'm six months pregnant. I have two other kids, ages 4 and 6.

My parents live with us. Their health is deteriorating.

I'm embarrassed to say that I'm uncomfortable about my parents' declining health. And so is my husband.

Is it best to shield my children (including the one on the way) from these realities of aging?

Response:

Short answer: No.

One of life's most precious blessings is the grandparent-grandchild relationship.

Grandparents can play a significant role in a child's development, including the child that you are expecting.

From the first moment that child will be held, bonds will be established with family members. If possible, this would include grandparents. They can play a vital role in a child's development.

From a family bonding perspective, it's wonderful that your parents live with you.

With respect to their deteriorating health, whenever feasible the elderly should be cared for at home. Here, the family can provide a nurturing environment.

But if adult children are uneasy about their parents' deteriorating health, they may not expose their children to this reality.

Remember that children take their cues from their parents' (or principal caregivers'/role models') behavior.

The result?

Children are invariably impacted by parental attitudes towards a grandparent's ill health.

Where possible, children should participate in caring for an ailing grandparent — whether in the home or in an institution.

This involvement keeps the family unit intact and enriched.

Follow Up Question

My 4 year old has started asking questions about her grandpa's health. Like "Why are you feeding grandma?"

My 6 year old wants to know, "How did Barker die?" (we had to put the dog down last month).

Honestly, I'd rather not discuss these things with them (or with my third child, who's likely to have similar questions as she develops.)

So I've been ignoring their questions or changing the subject...I don't know if that's the right thing to do. How should I answer these types of questions from my children?

Response:

Children's questions about aging should be addressed, carefully.

That said, it's not uncommon for parents to disapprove of or ignore their children's questions about aging and a grandparent's health. This reflects the parents' own embarrassment with this subject.

So how do moms and dads answer their children's questions?

Simply. Honestly. Age-appropriately.

Example:

"Why are you feeding grandma?"

Avoidance Answer:

"Grandma is tired."

Honest Answer:

"Grandma is sick [Alzheimer's] so she can't eat."

As to your 6 year old's question about Barker's death, parents need to be clear about their views on this sensitive subject.

Children deserve answers to their questions about the death of a grandparent, a pet, a friend, or anyone else.

Remember, children take what their parents say, **literally**.

Take your 6 year old's question, for example.

He asked:

"How did Barker die?"

Typical response from a parent:

"[insert dog's name] was put to sleep."

This type of response can cause children to have sleep problems.

Why?

Some children may worry that they will die when they sleep.

This is why probably why one 6 year old panicked when he was told that he would be "put to sleep" before surgery.

Words that are said to children matter. Choose your words **carefully**. Choose your words **wisely**.

How to be a positive role model for your children when it comes to their grandparents' ill health.

Your children can be enriched by being involved with their grandparents who have health challenges.

But turmoil, grief and shame about aging, sickness and death leads many parents to exclude their children from these challenges.

Your discomfort doesn't need to limit you, or stop you from including your children in their grandparents' life. You can learn to manage it. This is important, because **when children participate in the caring and concern for their aging grandparents, they learn a lot about life. Your children deserve to learn these lessons.**

So, why not start learning how to manage the emotional discomfort, **now**. That's better for you — and for your children.

Try This Exercise:

Using the blank spaces below, **write down every example of emotional discomfort — turmoil, grief, shame and guilt — that you can think of and a sensible, potential solution to it**.

Keep repeating the next three lines until you've worked through every emotional discomfort you can think of — even if it's a long list!

*When it comes to my parents' ailing health, I feel **turmoil** because*

_____

_____

But when I feel turmoil, I don't need to let it hold me back, or stop me from involving my children with caring for their grandparent.

I can tell myself something supportive and nurturing, like

_____

_____

*When it comes to my parents' ailing health, I feel **grief** because*

_____

_____

But when I feel grief, I don't need to let it hold me back, or stop me from involving my children with caring for their grandparent.

I can tell myself something supportive and nurturing, like

_____

_____

*When it comes to my parents' ailing health, I feel **shame** because*

_____

_____

But when I feel shame, I don't need to let it hold me back, or stop me from involving my children with caring for their grandparent.

I can tell myself something supportive and nurturing, like

_____

_____

*When it comes to my parents' ailing health, I feel **guilty** because*

_____

_____

But when I feel guilty, I don't need to let it hold me back, or stop me from involving my children with caring for their grandparent.

I can tell myself something supportive and nurturing, like

_____

_____

Once you've covered every emotional discomfort you can think of, if you're still feeling a bit uneasy, try this affirmation:

I am a loving daughter.

I am good parent.

I can take fine care of myself and my precious family. I am filled with love, gratitude and hope.

Question No. 9 — Positive Discipline

How To Teach Children To Make Good Decisions Beginning at Birth

"When I was growing up, my mother was bossy and always telling me what to do... like she was micromanaging me.

If I asked why I need to do some things, she would get mad.

Her answer was always: "Because I said so!"

Now, as I'm pregnant with my first daughter, I'm worried that my child won't like me, if I give her some direction on how to behave.

I don't think I want to tell her what to do because I don't want her to feel miserable like I did when I was growing up. I want her to be happy and to be my friend.

I'm excited for my daughter to arrive, but I think that raising a child nowadays is a challenge and some things in life are beyond a parent's control. Am I wrong for thinking this way?

Response:

You're not alone in thinking that environmental influences on children are beyond your control. Many parents think this way.

I disagree though.

When parents guide their children responsibly, this can have a powerful impact on child. They learn how to make sound choices, be self-respecting, and develop morals.

Children do need to receive instruction on what to do and when and how to do it. This is not the case with every single thing they do, every single moment of their lives, but there are many instances where the ideal would be that they are given at least two choices:

—You can have this or that, but you can't have this

—You can go here and you can do that, but you can't do this.

It is important that this approach be consistently implemented.

Be aware that your daughter is prone to emulate anything she's see and hears. This is why it is vital that you shield her from harmful influences.

How do you accomplish this?

With **careful supervision and guidance**.

This means sensibly monitoring what your child experiences.

It also means, unlike the experience you had while growing up, explaining to her in an age-appropriate way, why some behaviors are acceptable and others are not.

With this approach, you can teach your daughter how to make positive choices that keep her out of harm's way.

At what age do children learn to make good decisions?

Teaching and learning begins from the moment of birth.

"Isn't an newborn too young to learn to make choices," some parents have asked.

Another parent wondered:

"When my two year old wants to know, 'Why can't I have that?' isn't my child too young to be able to learn why some things are ok to have and others are not?"

It is vital that infants are shown what they can and cannot touch or play with.

As they get a little older, they tend to want everything.

Example:

Let's say, when your daughter is a little older, she is curious about toys. She wants to have all the toys that she sees.

Healthy parenting would look like this:

You would tell your daughter, with patience and kindness, what she can have, why she can have it.

You would also tell her what she cannot have and why she cannot have it.

The same approach would apply to what she eats and wears.

Children also need to be taught and to understand the difference between danger and safety.

As they grow older, they need to learn where they can and cannot go and parents need to explain to them why this is so.

Follow-Up Question

But if I start saying "No" a lot to my daughter when she's young, won't my "No's" be stifling her developing personality?

Response:

Short answer: No.

Children need a good frame of reference for their choice making (meaning: they need to be taught and know the difference between **right and wrong**, and between **acceptable and unacceptable behavior.**). Otherwise, by the time they reach adolescence, change may be difficult.

Talk to any parent who has tried to reeducate and discipline teenagers who have had their way and manipulated their family for 12 or 14 years. It is not easy!

"But my child won't like me…"

In terms of worrying that your child won't like you for saying "No," remember the following:

—**Being liked by one's child should not be the issue.**

—**What matters is that your child learns how to behave.**

Of course there are likely to be lots of things that she won't like or want to do while she growing up.

But your responsibility as a parent includes three critical factors:

1. Giving your child **explanations** for the behavior that you want her to engage in.

2. Insisting on **compliance**.

3. Applying appropriate **consequences** if necessary.

Listening to your child's ideas.

If, when your child gets to the age that she's able to — and wants to — express her reasons for or against doing something, it's important that you listen to what she has to say.

Listening doesn't automatically mean "giving in to."

That said, sometimes children learn from others (say, parents and teachers) about a better way to do something.

If the ideas that your child expresses are reasonable, by all means you should consider them. Regardless, it would be important to praise your child for her input.

Another Follow-Up Question

"My girlfriend has been strict with raising her 9-year-old. But she worries that he will rebel when he's with his friends. I worry about that too... if I'm strict with my daughter, will she rebel later?"

Response:

If you raise your child in a loving, disciplined home, she is likely to develop self-esteem and self-respect. Children who develop these characteristics tend not to rebel.

In essence, they respect their parents so they do not want to embarrass them by doing things that their parents have been taught them not to do. If these children find that are curious about something, they are likely to check with their parents before going ahead and getting involved with it.

Chaperoning

Whenever an activity that children are engaged in needs to be supervised, they should be chaperoned by a responsible adult.

Example:

Say your daughter is 7 years old, and she is playing with some of her friends in the backyard, then it would not be necessary for you, or another adult to whom you would entrust your daughter's care, to sit on the lawn and constantly supervise.

But if, say your daughter is 11 years old, and you allow her to go on an outing away from home, like to the mall or the movies, then it would be necessary for her to be chaperoned.

Keep Your Child Involved

It's important that you engage your child in age-appropriate learning.

Also make sure that she always has something constructive to do.

As she gets older, it can be extremely positive that she be involved with home upkeep.

Example:

Picking up after herself.

Chores should be required and time allowed for this task.

Example:

Doing the dishes.

How to avoid nagging.

The all-too typical parental nagging to enlist compliance with doing chores, can, and should be, avoided.

Ideally the whole family should convene at a family meeting. Here household responsibilities and chores can discussed and assigned.

It would be a good idea to create a list of the agreed-upon responsibilities. Post this list in a location where it can be easily seen.

Example:

On the refrigerator.

How consequences work

Another item that should be addressed at the family meeting has to do with what happens if children don't comply with what is required of them.

This is where consequences for non-compliance come into play.

These consequences should be predetermined — at the family meeting, for example.

This is important so that children know **ahead of time** what is expected of them. They also know **ahead of time** what will happen if they choose not to comply.

This is an excellent way to support a child in making positive choices and good decisions. The pending consequence is intended to serve as a **deterrent**. It can incentivize the child to make a positive choice so as to avoid a consequences for non-compliance.

Consequences should be strong enough to act as a deterrent, but not so severe (grounded for a year), that it is unreasonable and fosters resentment in the child.

Examples:

—Consequence = deterrent.

Child doesn't complete homework for the next school day. Consequence: cannot watch favorite TV show that evening.

—Consequence = too severe.

Child doesn't complete homework for the next school day. Consequence: cannot watch favorite TV show for the rest fo the year.

They'll Grow Out of It

"Teenagers will be teenagers. They'll grow out of it."

These remarks, or something similar, are ones I've heard often from parents of rebellious preteens.

This is an irresponsible attitude.

Generally speaking, it's not likely that these children are going to grow out of anything. Quite the opposite.

They run the risk of developing a pattern of negative behavior that could negatively impact them for the rest of their life.

All too often I've heard parents with troubled adult children lament:

"If I had only known that giving in to my kids while they were growing up, was priming them to be irresponsible adults who always want their way. I would definitely have done things differently."

Giving Your Child the Very Best

This was probably a longer answer to your question(s) than you might have expected. But making sure that your child gets the best opportunities to have a happy and productive life, is an enormous commitment.

I hope that you feel a little more confident now, knowing that with positive, loving discipline, and appropriate supervision, you can teach your child to make positive choices.

What this means for your child's future… and for the future of your parent-child relationship.

This means that your child can look forward to a productive future.

It also means that the two of you can enjoy a strong, healthy relationship with each other. A relationship that is based on mutual respect and love.

Visualization Exercise

Find a quiet, private space in your home where you can take 3 to 5 minutes of quiet, uninterrupted time.

Sit comfortably and close your eyes.

Take a deep breath in.

Exhale.

Now, imagine that you are holding your new baby girl in your arms.

You've just started to feed her.

As you do this, you're having to:

—Monitor how much is enough

—Handle cries for "more"

—Manage resistance

You accept this responsibility with confidence.

Visualize yourself affirming:

"My child is dependent on me to teach her how to manage her energy. Positive, loving discipline will support this learning "

"I will love and teach this precious child the best way I can."

When you're ready, open your eyes and enjoy feeling confident.

Question No. 10 — Safety

How To Teach Children Safety Skills That Build Confidence

"I'm expecting my third child. He will join two siblings - four-year-old Tyler, and Julie, 11 months.

I panic about keeping the kids safe at home, and I'm always "losing it" if it seems like they could be harmed — like when my youngest hit the dog, and I grabbed her and I yelled at her:

"Don't you ever hit the dog again!"

She looked at me with such fear... I can't get that image out of my mind. I don't want to be so explosive and scare my kids.

How can I teach my kids to be safe, including my third child, without losing my cool and panicking?"

Response:

First, you want to make sure that your environment is child-proof.

You also need to be supervising whatever they're doing to keep them safe.

Teaching safety begins early. Even very young children need to be taught how to stay out of harm's way.

Age-appropriate safety rules need to be established. When children follow rules, they typically feel a sense of achievement ("I can do this."). This can boost their confidence and self-esteem.

On the flip-side, when a parent's immediate reaction to a safety issue with a child is panic (e.g., yelling at your daughter), this can impact the child in two different ways:

— **The child's self-esteem and confidence could be damaged.**

How does this happen?

When parents project their own excessive fears onto their child, they tend to panic about the child's safety.

"Don't you ever hit the dog again!"

The parent's overreaction instills an unwarranted fear of the environment in the child.

—**The child could develop a false sense of confidence.**

What does that mean?

The child may defy the parent's rules and engage in risky behavior.

It's all about confidence.

Panic and confidence cannot co-exist.

Parents who react nervously and yell where safety is an issue with their child, invariably need to strengthen their confidence.

Imagine for a moment, that your confidence was stronger.

Here's how differently you could handle a safety issue:

Say you notice a pending danger — your four-year-old spilled something on the floor. You're understandably concerned that he may slip on the wet floor.

With your confidence intact, you could calmly guide your son away from the hazardous area.

You could then reassure him:

"I know you didn't spill on purpose. But you need to clean up the mess."

To avoid future spills, you could **patiently** show your son how to pour carefully.

You would also need to **supervise** him *particularly* closely.

Why?

Because at his age, children typically want to assert their independence and try to do things for themselves.

With your confidence intact, here's how differently you could handle the safety issue with your daughter:

When you see her hitting the dog, you realize that the dog might retaliate by biting her. You then act quickly, but calmly, to make sure she's out of harm's way... making sure her and the dog are separated.

You help her to manage her impulsiveness by explaining:

"We don't hit dogs."

This is a **calm, sensible** approach to teaching your children safety skills.

The result?

This approach fosters their ability to **confidently** make choices that keep them safe.

Replacing Fear With Confidence

No matter how many times you've reacted nervously when your children's safety has been at issue, and whether you feel you may have dampened their confidence, it's never too late to do better, and emphasize safety in a way that fosters self-esteem.

You Can Begin To Reframe Your Nervous Reactions and Commit to Positive Change for the Better ... With These Affirmations.

Even though I panicked when

_____

_____

I know how to do better.

I can

_____

_____

Even though

_____

_____

happened when I identified pending danger, I can do better.

I can teach my child

_____

_____

Even though I've always had a tough time with

_____

_____

I can change and grow.

From now on, I will

_____

_____

Even though it's hard for me to

_____

_____

I know that my child deserves to feel confident. To have high self-esteem.

From now on, I will

_____

_____

Closing thoughts on safety and self-esteem.

Your question invited an important opportunity:

— To explore how to foster self-esteem, which begins in infancy by teaching children about safety as they test limits and develop the courage to meet their challenges.

As you teach your children about safety in a confident way, you are offering them a precious opportunity to build self-esteem.

Why?

Because think about what happens **when children feel safe:**

Their confidence grows.

Confidence offers children two very precious gifts:

1. The ability to develop courage to meet life's challenges.

2. The ability to take pride in their achievements.

Wrap up:

That's the end of the Question and Answer portion of this book. We covered quite a range of topics… from getting back in shape post-birth to teaching children confidence-building safety skills.

I hope you enjoyed it.

Remember: you are not the first person to become a parent.

And even if you're raising your child on your own, you are never "alone."

There's so much help out there. Take it, if you feel you need it.

A FEW FINAL WORDS

Parenting Can Be a Challenge, but It Doesn't Have To Be Complicated.

Right now, before your child arrives, your job is to take excellent care of your body and emotions, prepare your home, strengthen your bond with your partner, if you have one, and most of all ...

Get to know yourself better, so that you can avoid some of the unhelpful patterns that may have been forged in your past.

And once your child arrives, your job is simply to teach them right from wrong — with firm, fair guidance, consistently applied with love.

Do that, and you can set your child up for a beautiful future. And you can have an equally beautiful journey, as a parent.

WHAT'S NEXT?

RESOURCES... TO KEEP LEARNING AND GROWING

I hope you've enjoyed this Life Guide. It is "technically" complete, but I wanted to give you some **more resources on self-care, parenting** (looking ahead after giving birth)**, and success in life** ... in case you'd like to continue the learning and the growing.

Here are some of my favorites — articles I've authored,[1] another Life Guide I created, and inspiring insights I shared when I was interviewed by a reporter from the Weekend Today Show, to savor at your leisure.

Enjoy to the fullest ...

---

[1] All articles referenced in this section were published online.

SELF-CARE

6 Self-Sabotaging Habits You Need To Drop Right Now
— Published on Mind Body Green.

In this article, I encourage readers to do a "habit audit." This means: Paying attention to whether they're sabotaging themselves by being mean to themselves, saying "Yes" when they really mean "No," or blaming their parents for how their life turned out for example,… and to drop these habits if they're present.

https://www.mindbodygreen.com/0-14014/6-selfsabotaging-habits-you-need-to-drop-right-now.html

The Life Guides.

I wrote this series of guidebooks to help you successfully navigate some of life's trickiest challenges. Each e-book includes educational information sourced from my 30+ years of coaching and counseling in the field of emotional wellness, exercises to help you release stress, anger, and insecurity, and an audio companion that you can listen to on-the-go. Available here.

http://drsuzannegelb.com/life-guides-by-dr_gelb/

The Life Guide on How To Reach Your Ideal Weight — Through Kindness Not Craziness,

Inside this Life Guide, you will find empirically-proven steps to help start treating your body with the care and respect it deserves.

Because once you do that, returning to your ideal weight can happen naturally, without self-punishment or craziness.

For pregnant moms who worry about how they will be able to lose the weight they gained during their pregnancy — and keep that weight off — this guide can be your best friend… especially because as you read this guide, you can learn how to build confidence (and feel sexy!) while you're on a weight-loss journey.

http://drsuzannegelb.com/life-guide-ideal-weight/

Praise for Dr. Gelb's Life Guides

"Dr. Gelb has a gentle spirit that instantly makes you feel like you've come home. The depth of her wisdom is undeniable, her curiosity is insatiable and her love is palpable. These qualities make her the perfect guide for life. In the pages of the Life Guides you will find practical and proven processes to support you in living your great life. Whether it's heart-centered wisdom on navigating the dating world, love-based strategies for becoming a parent, or reaching your ideal weight through kindness, Dr. Gelb's Life Guides are gifts to be treasured."

— Dr. Gemma Stone, Psychologist, Mentor, Author

"Learning how to love yourself and treat yourself kindly — even when your life, career, body, and relationships aren't 'totally perfect' — is one of the hardest things to do. Dr. Suzanne Gelb breaks down the art of self-love into practical steps. No woo-woo vagueness. Just easy-to-follow exercises pulled from her 28-year career in the field. If you're looking for practicality and effectiveness, these Life Guides are a steal of a deal."

—Susan Hyatt, Master Certified Life Coach, Published Author

"This Life Guide came at the perfect time. My two fears about losing weight were dispelled immediately and it was such a relief

to know that I can start looking after myself without the worry of going to the gym or going on another desperate diet.

The audio helped re-frame the reasons why I've let my weight spiral out of control and the work book helped me set out an action plan. Thanks Dr. Gelb for your Life Guide, here's to a happier, healthier life."

—Amanda Herbert, photographer

If You Want to Make Tomorrow Less Stressful—Start Tonight
— Published on The Muse

You can find this article on my column on the Muse. The column is called, "Be Well At Work."

The stress management tips that I cover in this article, apply to all aspects of life, not just a workday. That said, parenting is one of the most important "jobs."

This article is a relevant read if you want to learn how to manage your emotions and keep your stress levels in check.

It includes suggestions for stress-relieving activities that take place after-work and an empowering morning affirmation to set the tone for a positive day. You'll also learn about the importance of scheduling deep breathing breaks during the day, and how to do an emotional inventory (and an emotional release, if needed) at the end of the day.

https://www.themuse.com/advice/if-you-want-to-make-tomorrow-less-stressfulstart-tonight

Side note: The Muse is an award-winning online career resource, with over 4 million quality, professional members. I'm honored to have received the praise below, from Adrian Granzella Larssen, Editor-in-Chief, in response to an article I wrote for The Muse:

"Wow! This is fantastic stuff. You're clearly incredible at what you do, and I'm so thrilled to share your advice with our audience!"

You Are The Best Investment You'll Ever Make
— Published on my column ,"All Grown-Up," onPsychology Today.

In this article, I address ways to invest in ourselves and I present some questions about self-investment practices that readers can reflect on.

Readers are encouraged to make a list of doable ways they can invest in themselves. I offer suggestions about what to include on their list.

https://www.psychologytoday.com/blog/all-grown/201511/you-are-the-best-investment-youll-ever-make

PARENTING

It Starts With You. How To Raise Happy, Successful Children By Being The Best Role Model You Can Possibly Be — A Guidebook, by Dr. Gelb

This book contains educational exercises and tips drawn from my career in the field of emotional wellness with over 30 years of experience.

—As you make your way through the pages of this book, you can learn how to raise happy, successful children who have every possible chance to grow up and become happy, successful adults.

—You'll learn about some of the more common problem areas that parents run into as they're raising their child — such as, defiance, manipulation, underachievement, perfectionism, procrastination, bad manners, shyness, overweight and much more.

I offer constructive and practical ways to address these types challenges that parents may encounter with their children.

Parents-to-be who read this book can get a head start on not only (a) being aware of these potential problems. but also on (b) how to avoid and prevent these potentially troublesome issues for occurring in the first place.

Author's Note: *It Starts With You* can be a nice companion to *How to Get Ready To Be A New Parent*. The former is a 205 page resource that offers an in-depth focus largely on parents as role models, whereas the latter is a 118 page guidebook that focuses on preparing to be a new parent.

https://www.amazon.com/Starts-You-Successful-Becoming-Guidebook/dp/0692647392/ref=tmm_pap_swatch_0?_encoding=UTF8&qid=1553581148&sr=1-4

The Life Guide On How To Get Your Kids To Cooperate -- And Help Them Become the BEST Grown-Ups They Can Be

Before you tear your hair out, read this practical, encouraging guidebook. Peace: right ahead!

http://drsuzannegelb.com/get-kids-cooperate/

The Life Guide On Helping Your Teen Make Healthy Choices About Dating and Sex

A must read for parents of tweens and teens.

http://drsuzannegelb.com/helping-teen-make-healthy-choices-dating-sex/

Three Lessons You Must Teach Your Kids. (The sooner the better. But it's never too late)
— Published on Dr. Gelb's column, "All Grown Up" on Psychology Today

This article covers certain essential lessons that parents must teach their children, especially if their children are uncooperative. Since that is a learned behavior that can be unlearned, these lessons should be implemented at the earliest opportunity.

Topics that I write about in this article include choices and consequences, integrity, and learning to befriend the word, "No."

https://www.psychologytoday.com/us/blog/all-grown/201503/parents-three-lessons-you-must-teach-your-kids

Why "Bribing" Your Child With Treats... Doesn't Work. And What Does
— Published on Dr. Gelb's column, "All Grown Up" on Psychology Today

Many parents bribe their children to entice them to cooperate. As noted in the article, this is problematic because then a child is not likely to ever do something simply because it's the right thing to do—the child is always going to want some form of "compensation" for their action.

This is simply not the way the world works, and parents aren't doing their children any favors by encouraging this "bribery-action" formula.

In this article, I lay out for parents some simple ways to gain their child's cooperation without having to resort to bribing. Topics covered include: rules, consequences, communication, progress charts, and the importance of parental consistency.

Raising Kids Who Love Reading and Devour Books Voraciously
— Published on my column, "All Grown Up" on Psychology Today

In this article, I suggest ways to effectively prompt children to read more, including the child who is especially resistant to reading.

In order for parents to determine what might spark their child's curiosity about / enthusiasm for reading, I pose five questions for parents to consider. Topics covered in the questions include their child's: favorite movies or TV shows, passion, role models and heroes, and the impact of parents' reading behavior on their child.

https://www.psychologytoday.com/us/blog/all-grown/201507/raising-kids-who-love-reading-devour-books-voraciously

"Mommy, Do You Love Your Blog More Than Me?" What To Do if Your Child Feels in Competition With Your Work
— Published on The Huffington Post

Many working parents feel conflicted about how to balance work demands with effective parenting and giving their children adequate attention. A common conclusion — it's not possible to balance work and family life so that neither is shortchanged.

I disagree.

In this article you'll learn how it is possible to be involved with your work, while still conveying to your child that they are your number one priority, so that they can feel secure in your love for them, even when you're fully engaged in your work.

https://www.huffpost.com/entry/mommy-do-you-love-your-blog-more-than-me-what-to_b_58dde22ce4b0fa4c095987f2

3 Ways to Stop Your Teen From Making Risky Choices
— Published on The Huffington Post

The extent to which teens and pre-teens don't do things to endanger themselves (and potentially their entire future) is highly correlated to the types of choices they make.

To this end, in this article I write about three things that parents can do to keep their children safe. The list includes supervising dates, monitoring online activity, as well as rules, and consistent implementation of consequences (if necessary).

As I point out in the article, your kids may not like you for adhering to the items on the above-mentioned list. But when they are adults, they may very well look back on how you parented them, and feel deep gratitude.

Good Parenting Isn't Complicated — Here's Why
—Published on Maria Shriver

Imagine if parenting was simply a matter of caring for your child in the same way that you would care for yourself.

Now don't imagine that. Instead, accept that as fact. Accept that as true. Because in essence, it is true.

But then there's the problem that many parents simply don't know how to care for themselves when it comes to their emotions, self-respect, self-love, and the like. Their parents didn't teach them how to relate to themselves in this way. They in turn don't teach their child. And so the cycle of lack of self-care is passed on from one generation to the next.

But it is possible to change this pattern. To break the cycle. To learn to reparent oneself, and in turn, to be a better parent to one's child/ren.

This is what this particular article is all about. To read more, click on the link below.

bit.ly/1QlQQsE

7 Dangerous Lessons We Need To Stop Teaching Our Kids
— Published on Mind Body Green

Kids are smart and perceptive. And parents, if you're doing 1 of these 7 no-no's ... they'll notice. That's why I wrote this article . Over the years, I've observed countless parents role-modeling behaviors for their children, that were sending a negative message.

Example:

Parents who overeat or drink too much, are sending a message to their children that it's really alright to disrespect your body.

The thing is... (and I'm not making excuses for parents with what I'm about to say) sometimes parents simply aren't aware of the messages they're sending to their children.

That's where this article can help. You can read about some of the dangerous lessons that parents may pass onto children, and you'll no longer be unaware.

Some of the dangerous lessons that are covered in this article include: a relationship with technology is more important than interacting with people, if you cooperate, you'll get a cookie [or some type of food treat], and what other people want is more important than what you want.

https://www.mindbodygreen.com/0-14586/7-dangerous-lessons-we-need-to-stop-teaching-our-kids.html

Spring Cleaning for Your Life [Part 1/3]
— Published on The Huffington Post

This article is part of a series on tidying up our inner world – I call this, "Spring Cleaning for Your Life." It contains a checklist for parents and kids that can help you to create an even more peaceful, productive dynamic at home!

Topics on the checklist include:

—Household chores
—Consequences
—Handling stress and frustration
—Bedtime
—Social Media
—Giving back to the community

https://www.huffpost.com/entry/spring-cleaning-for-your_n_7253908

Time-Out. Getting the Most Out of This Popular Discipline Tactic
— Published in Family Advocate, Vol. 30, No. 1 (Summer 2007) American Bar Association

This is a powerful technique to implement positive discipline and help children to improve the way they behave — but only if implemented properly.

So why have so many parents shared with me over the years, that Time-Out doesn't work for them? Because it is not being implemented effectively. Why not?

Instead of being used as a learning opportunity for a child who is misbehaving, it is not uncommon for parents to use Time-Out as a form of punishment. This can cause a child to feel ashamed, fearful or criticized.

This is why, in this article I lay out some tips for parents so they can understand Time-Out and its constructive purpose, and they can get some ideas to use it correctly.

Then, instead of resorting to negative behaviors such as yelling and screaming at their children to try to get them to cooperate, parents can properly implement this simple tool that can help their children to think about their behavior, start over, and make better choices — a win-win for everyone.

https://bit.ly/2FdxXYy

When the Other Parent Doesn't Play Fair
— Published in Family Advocate, Vol. 30, No. 1 (Summer 2007) American Bar Association

One of the most frustrating aspects of being a divorced co-parent, is when one parent plays hardball, so to speak, and makes co-parenting extremely difficult.
Examples:

— The resistant parent may not show up for a scheduled visitation. Not only does this frustrate the other parent, but it is also a let-down for the child.
—The resistant parent may try to turn a child against the non-offending parent, by bad-mouthing that parent to the child.

This article offers suggestions on how the non-offending parent can effectively manage the challenges of dealing with an uncooperative co-parent, so that the best interests of the child can be prioritized.

bit.ly/1QmYYpq

Raising an Organized Child In a Blended Family
— Published in Family Advocate, Vol. 36, No. 1 (Summer 2013) American Bar Association

There can be many challenges, changes and adjustments that children (and parents) face when there is significant life change, such as shifting from a single-parent household to a blended family household.

There's a lot for parents to manage and juggle. But with proper role-modeling the blended family dynamic presents a tremendous opportunity for parents to teach their children a critical life skill — how to be organized. This means that children can develop good planning skills, a sharp ability to focus, and the ability to be productive and accomplish things.

Topics that are covered in this article include:

—Benefits of parents being organized and modeling this behavior
—Importance of family time
—Creating routines
—Implementing an organizational chart
—Teaching time management
—The power of praise

https://bit.ly/2HJgxFW

HOW TO LIVE A SUCCESSFUL LIFE

How to Succeed Everywhere: 10 Tips for Balance at Work, Home, in Relationships
— Written by Shelby Marra, published online on NBC's Today.

Learn my top ten tips on how women [can apply to anyone] can become high achievers in whatever they do — at work, in romance and as a parent. For partners, the romance section in this article, can be especially insightful.

https://www.today.com/health/how-become-high-achieving-woman-work-your-relationship-parent-t33071

Side note: As my colleague, friend, and gifted writing teacher, Alex Franzen said: *"THIS IS AMAZING! Being interviewed by a reporter from NBC's Today Show? Uh, that's the big leagues!"*

Yes, that's what happened. Shelby Marra with NBC's Today Show in New York, requested an interview with me so that she could write this article featuring me, for TODAY.com's Successful Women series.

How Successful People Do More in 24 Hours Than the Rest of Us Do in a Week
— Published on Newsweek; also published on The Muse

The content in this article is bound to inspire. Some of the topics I cover include: "Fully Commit," "Ban 'Friendly Interruptions' at All Costs," "Hang With Fellow Super-Achievers," and "Prevent Emotions From Building." It takes a self-loving person to take this type of positive action to further their success.

https://www.newsweek.com/career/how-successful-people-do-more-24-hours-rest-us-do-week

ABOUT THE AUTHOR

Dr. Suzanne Gelb, Ph.D., J.D. is a psychologist, life coach, TV commentator and author.

Dr. Gelb's inspiring insights on personal growth have been featured on more than 200 radio programs, 260 TV interviews, and online on Time, Newsweek, Forbes, The Huffington Post, NBC's Today, Psychology Today, The Daily Love, Positively Positive, Mind Body Green, The Muse and many other places.

Dr. Gelb served as a parenting expert writer for Hawaii Parent magazine for over 14 years and appeared regularly on television to share tips on a parenting segment for 6 years.

As a contributing writer to Psychology Today, where she has her own column, "All Grown Up," Dr. Gelb has written articles on parenting, including, **10 Vital Life Lessons to Teach Your Kids Before They Turn 10**, and **10 Ways to Become the Parent Your Children Really Need**. Her powerful article, **How To Do An Effective Timeout**, was published on The Huffington Post.

She believes that it is never too late to become the person — and parent — you want to be. Strong. Confident. Calm. Creative. Free of all of the burdens that have held you back — no matter what has happened in the past.

To learn more, visit DrSuzanneGelb.com.

OTHER BOOKS BY THE AUTHOR

It Starts With You – How to Raise Happy, Successful Children by Becoming the Best Role-Model You Can Possibly Be. A Guidebook For Parents.

How to Get Your Kids to Cooperate and Help Them Become the Best Grown-Ups They Can Be. (A Life Guide.)

Helping Your Teen Make Healthy Choices About Dating and Sex. (A Life Guide.)

How to Forgive the One Who Hurt You Most. (A Life Guide.)

How to Deal With People Who Drive You Absolutely Nuts. (A Life Guide.)

Aging With Grace, Strength and Self-Love. (A Life Guide.)

How to Navigate Being Single and Savor Your Dating Adventure. (A Life Guide.)

The Love Tune-Up: How to Amp Up the Love That's Naturally Inside You to Enjoy Happy, Healthy Relationships.

How to Rekindle That Spark and Create the Relationship and Sex Life That You Want. (A Life Guide.)

How to Find Work That You Love When You're Stuck in a Job That You Hate. (A Life Guide.)

How to Reach Your Ideal Weight Through Kindness, Not Craziness. (A Life Guide.)

Welcome Home: Release Addiction and Return to Love.

How to Care for Yourself When You're a Caregiver for Somebody Else. (A Life Guide.)

Real Men Don't Vacuum. And Other Misguided Myths That Cause Conflict in Relationships.

INDEX[2]

A

affirmations, 16, 25, 48, 79
age-appropriate, 50, 53, 60, 68
anxious and overwhelmed, 1
avoid nagging, 73

B

be a healthy role model, 47
body, 24, 26, 30, 31, 84, 86, 87, 94

C

chaperoning, 72
childcare, 34
childhood conditioning, 57
chores, 35, 72, 73
commit to making changes, 16
commitment, 2, 9, 29, 75
concerns, 5
confident, 31, 33, 75, 76, 82, 99
consequences for non-compliance, 13, 41, 73
controlling co-parent, 56
couple(s), 3, 59

D

delegate tasks, 40
developmental milestones, 45-46

E

effective parent, 13, 92
enjoy, 1, 2, 42, 45, 51, 75, 76
excited, 1, 6, 45, 56, 67

F

fears, 8, 20, 23, 78, 87
feeling, 8, 1, 2, 5, 7, 19, 21, 23, 32, 40, 66, 76
fill-in-the-blank worksheets, 4
fun, 27

G

gathering support, 8, 28
gentleness, 25
getting back in shape, 30
grandparents, 60, 63
guilt-free parenting, 40

---

[2] The page numbers in this index refer to the printed version of this book.

H

happy and excited, 1
healthy parenting, 68
helpful pattern, 12
huge life commitment, 2

L

learning and growing, 8
listening to your child's ideas, 69

M

make a plan, 8, 24
manipulate, 12, 56

N

navigate, 7
navigate the parenting journey, 7, 1, 2
nourishing, 25, 29, 30

O

organize and prepare, 26
other books, 9, 99
overcoming fear, 21
overprotective, 39

P

parental instincts, 47
parenting intentions, 8
parenting patterns, 4, 13, 14
patience and care, 25
pent-up emotion, 24, 26

positive change, 79
positive discipline, 13, 14, 41, 66, 94
professional resources, 30

Q

quick reference guide, 3

R

realistic, 25, 40
reasonable rules, 13, 41
reframe, 16, 79
refresher course, 3
relax, 7, 1, 2, 45
releasing stress, 25
resources, 8, 11, 30, 85

S

safety, 76-78
self-assessment, 36
self-care planning worksheet, 4
self-care practices, 25
self-esteem, 30, 33, 35, 38, 51, 52, 54, 70, 76, 77, 79, 80, 81
self-nurturing exercise, 31
self-talk, 4
setting an intention, 9
sibling rivalry, 50, 53
single parent, 38
soothing your fears, 8, 20
stay home or go to work, 33
stressed, 24
stuck, 19
subconscious patterns, 18
super-parent, 40
supervision and guidance, 67

support, 8, 7, 28, 30, 31, 34, 47, 58, 72, 74, 86

U

unconditional love, 2
unhelpful pattern, 12, 15, 83
unified parenting team, 3
unresolved feelings, 11

V

visualization exercise, 54, 74

W

weight-gain, 30
well-organized, 40
well-rested, 28
work demands, 35, 91
worksheets, 4
worried, 2
writing exercise, 5, 9, 42

www.ingramcontent.com/pod-product-compliance
Lightning Source LLC
Chambersburg PA
CBHW020144130526
44591CB00030B/198